Cambridge Experience Readers

Level 3

Series editor: Nicholas Tims

Alone!

Jane Rollason

CAMBRIDGE
UNIVERSITY PRESS

CAMBRIDGE
UNIVERSITY PRESS

University Printing House, Cambridge CB2 8BS, United Kingdom

One Liberty Plaza, 20th Floor, New York, NY 10006, USA

477 Williamstown Road, Port Melbourne, VIC 3207, Australia

4843/24, 2nd Floor, Ansari Road, Daryaganj, Delhi – 110002, India

79 Anson Road, #06–04/06, Singapore 079906

José Abascal 56, 1º – 28003 Madrid, Spain

Cambridge University Press is part of the University of Cambridge.

It furthers the University's mission by disseminating knowledge in the pursuit of education, learning and research at the highest international levels of excellence.

www.cambridge.org
Information on this title: www.cambridge.org/9788483236826

First published 2011

40 39 38 37 36 35 34 33 32 31 30 29 28 27 26

Printed in Spain by GraphyCems

ISBN 978-84-832-3682-6 Paperback; legal deposit: M-25365-2011

Illustrations by Paul Fisher Johnson

Edited by James Bean

Audio recording by Mark Smith Sound Engineering

Exercises by Jane Rollason

Cover image by Zoográfico

The publishers would like to thank Paul Price-Smith and James Bean of ILTS for their excellent management and editing of this title.

Contents

People in the story

Hannah Frost: a sixteen-year-old girl
Alfie Frost: Hannah's older brother
Mrs Violet Frost: Hannah's mother
Mr Henry Frost: Hannah's father
Marnie Moran: a woman who works for the Frost family
Grace Moran: Marnie's sixteen-year-old daughter
Leo Zimmerman: a young bank worker
Mr Miller: a rich man who owns a bank in Southampton
Daisy: a girl who works for the Miller family

BEFORE YOU READ

1 Look at the cover and the pictures in the first chapter. Answer the questions.

1 When do you think this story happens?

....

2 Do you know the story of the ship *Titanic*? What happened to it?

....

3 Who has a ticket to travel on the *Titanic*?

....

Introduction

Life in 1912

This story begins in an English town called Southampton in 1912. Southampton is by the sea, and big ships sailed from there to the United States. Around this time, many families were moving from Europe to the US. They wanted to start new lives in a new country.

Life in 1912 was different from life today. There were some cars, but most people travelled by carriage. Carriages were pulled by horses. Telephones were very new things then, and only a few people in England had them. Ships sent radio messages using a telegraph machine. Medicine and hospitals were not as good as they are today. Many people caught typhoid fever, and some died from it.

British money in 1912 was pounds and pence, as it is today. One British pound was worth five US dollars. A loaf of bread cost three pence and the cheapest ticket on the ship *Titanic* cost three pounds.

Chapter 1

A ticket on the *Titanic*

'Mrs Frost, are you ready?' called Marnie, from the front door. 'The carriage is here.'

'I'm nearly ready,' Hannah's mother called back. Then she turned to her daughter. 'You know I hate leaving you, my love, but you're too weak to travel. The doctor says you must rest for another three weeks.'

'And if I don't get better ...?' said Hannah.

'You will get better,' said Mrs Frost. She sat on Hannah's bed and took her hand. 'Remember, Dr Mason will visit you every day. Marnie will look after you. Then you can join us.'

'But I could come with you and rest on the ship.'

'Hannah, you've had typhoid fever. You were very ill and the doctor says you aren't ready,' said her mother.

'I can't believe you're leaving me on my own!' cried Hannah. 'All the family will be in America except me!'

'Don't behave like a child, Hannah,' said her mother. 'You're sixteen – a young woman. And you won't be on your own – Marnie's here. She's a part of the family.' Then Mrs Frost added quietly, 'Anyway, I have to go.'

'Why do you have to go now?' asked Hannah.

Before Mrs Frost could answer, Hannah's brother Alfie came into the room.

'Marnie needs you in the kitchen, Mother,' he said.

'I'll be back in a minute,' said Mrs Frost to Hannah, going downstairs.

'Come and sit by the window,' said Alfie to Hannah. 'You can wave to us from there.'

Hannah walked slowly to the chair by the window. Alfie put a blanket around her and hugged her.

'I wish you were coming with us,' he said, 'but Mother won't wait. And I can't let her travel alone.'

'You shouldn't go without me,' said Hannah.

'You're just thinking about yourself, Hannah,' said Alfie. 'You were away at school when the trouble started and since then, you've been ill in bed. You don't know how hard it's been for Mother out there.' He looked out of the window. 'Her friends won't speak to her and she's afraid the police will come for her too. We have to go now – before she falls ill.'

'Why did Father have to run away?' Hannah asked. 'Fathers should look after their families – not run away.'

'Hannah!' said Alfie. 'The police were looking for him. They still are. He had to go.'

'If he hasn't done anything, why do the police want him?' she said.

'Don't talk like that, Hannah,' said Alfie. His usual smile was gone. 'You know he hasn't done anything. You know he's innocent[1].'

'I'm sorry,' said Hannah, not looking at her brother. 'Of course he's innocent.'

They heard someone on the stairs.

'Ssh!' said Alfie to his sister.

Mrs Frost came in. 'Now, Hannah,' she said. 'I'm going to give your money and ticket to Marnie. I've paid the rent[2] on this house for the next four weeks. You've got two bags to bring – Alfie and I are taking everything else. Your dresses are in the big bag, and I've hidden your valuable things under your nightdresses in the small bag.'

'You've thought of everything,' said Hannah.

'Do you want to see your ticket before I take it down to Marnie?' asked her mother.

‘Yes, let’s see it,’ said Hannah, smiling now. ‘How exciting!’

‘You’re travelling on a White Star ship,’ said Mrs Frost. ‘When you arrive in New York, go to the White Star office with Marnie. We’ll meet there.’

‘You’re lucky,’ said Alfie. ‘You’re going on a new ship – they say it’s the best ship in the world.’

‘Miss Hannah Frost,’ Hannah read from the ticket. ‘Southampton to New York City. White Star Line. Sailing: 10th April 1912. Second Class. Ship: RMS *Titanic*.’

‘We’ll eat at the best restaurant in New York when you arrive, Hannah,’ said Alfie.

‘Oh yes!’ cried Hannah.

‘That’ll be lovely,’ said Mrs Frost. ‘Now, Alfie, I think we must go.’

Hannah hugged and kissed her mother and brother.

‘Be brave, Hannah,’ said Mrs Frost.

Hannah stayed at the window. She watched her brother carry the last case out of the house and give it to the carriage driver. Then Mrs Frost came out.

On the other side of the street, two well-dressed women were walking by. When they saw Mrs Frost, they stopped and shouted at her. One waved her umbrella angrily. Mrs Frost turned and looked up at Hannah's window, and Hannah saw the sadness in her mother's eyes.

Finally the carriage drove away. Hannah started to cry. First her father had left her, and now her mother and brother were leaving her. It was a long way across the ocean. Her eyes were still wet when Marnie came into her room.

'Don't cry, Miss Hannah,' she said. 'We'll see them again next month.'

'They've left me alone,' said Hannah.

'You don't realise how lucky you are,' said Marnie. She sounded angry. 'I'd like a new life in America too. But after I take you there I'm coming back to Southampton. I'll be back here without a job.'

And she went downstairs.

Chapter 2

The red book

Two hours later, Hannah was still sitting in the chair by the window. Marnie came in.

'Miss Hannah?' said Marnie. 'Why are you still in that chair?'

'I think I fell asleep,' said Hannah. Her blanket was on the floor and her body was shaking with cold. 'Why didn't you come up earlier?'

'There's a lot to do downstairs,' said Marnie. 'Let's get you into bed.'

'I had a terrible dream,' said Hannah. 'I dreamed that Father was in prison. I was shouting outside his window, but he couldn't hear me.'

'I haven't got time for dreams,' said Marnie. 'I'll bring up your supper and hot chocolate and then you must sleep.'

Hannah was soon fast asleep again in her bed.

When Dr Mason visited the next day, he was worried.

'Hannah, you look tired,' he said. 'You must get stronger before you leave for America. Try walking around the house. Go into the garden and get some fresh air.'

So for the next month, Hannah followed Dr Mason's advice.

Towards the end of the month, Marnie's daughter Grace came to stay. Grace was the same age as Hannah, and each morning the two girls went out for walks together.

Dr Mason made his final visit on 9th April, and he was pleased with Hannah.

'You're well enough to travel,' he told her. 'I'm going away myself this evening, so I can't come down to the *Titanic* with you tomorrow. I've got some family business in Liverpool.'

'Thank you for everything, Doctor,' said Hannah.

'Have a wonderful life in America, Hannah,' he said.

Grace and Hannah helped Marnie pack her cases.

'I hope you won't feel too sad tomorrow, Grace,' said Hannah.

'What do you mean, Miss Hannah?' said Grace.

'When you say goodbye to your mother ... when we get on the ship,' said Hannah.

'Oh, yes ... I see what you mean,' said Grace, laughing nervously.

'Grace is going back to her job after the *Titanic* sails,' said Marnie. 'She'll be too busy to think about me.'

They put Marnie's cases by the front door. The ship tickets and money were on the table in the sitting room.

After dinner, Hannah went up to her room for the last time. Marnie brought up a cup of hot chocolate.

'Here,' she said to Hannah. 'Drink this quickly and try to get to sleep. We've got an early start in the morning.'

'Isn't it exciting, Marnie?' said Hannah. 'In ten days' time, we'll be in New York!'

'Yes, Miss Hannah,' said Marnie, turning to leave.

'You don't sound very excited,' said Hannah.

'It's just a journey for me,' said Marnie. 'Remember, I'm coming back to Southampton after a week over there.'

'But you'll see New York – the Statue of Liberty, all the tall buildings ...'

Downstairs, the doorbell rang.

'I'll answer that,' said Marnie. 'Goodnight, Miss Hannah.'

As she started to drink her chocolate, Hannah thought about Marnie. When Hannah was younger, Marnie had been kind – always smiling and laughing. Then Hannah went away to school, and Marnie changed. She wasn't as friendly any more. Perhaps on the journey to America, Hannah would ask her why.

Hannah heard the front door of the house close.

'This chocolate isn't very nice. It tastes strange,' she thought, looking into her cup. 'I'll go and make another cup.'

Halfway down the stairs, she stopped. Marnie was talking to a man in the sitting room. Hannah knew the man's voice. It was Mr Miller. Her father had worked at Mr Miller's bank, before the trouble started.

'... here's your money, Marnie,' Mr Miller was saying. 'Well done! After you put those false accounts[3] in Frost's desk in place of the real accounts for last year, there was nothing he could do. But remember to keep your mouth shut.'

'Yes, of course,' said Marnie. 'What's that red book?'

'I keep a book like this every year. This one is for 1911,' said Mr Miller. 'I've got everything in here – names and addresses of customers[4], copies of the false accounts and Frost's real accounts.'

'What if the police find it?' said Marnie. 'Doesn't it show that Mr Frost is innocent?'

'They won't find it,' laughed Mr Miller. 'I keep it with me all the time. And don't forget I'm an important man in this town. I have many friends in the Southampton Police!'

Hannah was suddenly feeling unwell, but she moved quietly down to the bottom stair. Now she could see Mr Miller through the half-open door. There was a small, fat book in his hand. It was red, with the year '1911' in gold on the front.

'Why don't you burn it?' Hannah heard Marnie say.

'Because it's worth a lot of money to me,' said Mr Miller. 'Many people put money in our bank – and it wasn't always their money. I've got their names in here and I can make trouble for them. Information is money. If I ever need to—'

'Mother!' cried a voice behind Hannah.

Hannah turned to see Grace behind her on the stairs.

The sitting room door opened wide. Mr Miller and Marnie came towards Hannah.

'What did you hear?' shouted Mr Miller.

Their angry faces started to go around and around.

'The chocolate ...' Hannah started to say. And then she fell to the floor, unconscious[5].

LOOKING BACK

1 Check your answers to *Before you read* on page 4.

ACTIVITIES

2 Complete the sentences with the names in the box.

Mrs Frost	Mr Frost	~~Hannah~~
Alfie	Marnie	Dr Mason

1 ......Hannah...... has had typhoid fever.
2 .... is travelling to America with Mrs Frost.
3 .... will visit Hannah every day for three weeks.
4 .... is afraid the police will come for her.
5 Hannah says that .... has run away.
6 .... is going to travel with Hannah to New York.

3 Match the two parts of the sentences.

1 Hannah can't go with her mother and brother because [b]
2 Hannah's father went to America because [ ]
3 Dr Mason tells Hannah to walk and get fresh air so that [ ]
4 Dr Mason can't come down to the *Titanic* because [ ]
5 Marnie isn't excited about going to New York because [ ]

a he's going to Liverpool.
~~b~~ she isn't well enough to travel.
c the police were looking for him.
d she's coming back to England after a week.
e she'll be strong enough to travel to America.

4 Are the sentences true (*T*) or false (*F*)?

1 Marnie became less friendly after Hannah went away to school. T
2 Hannah goes downstairs because she hears a man's voice. F
3 Hannah's father worked at Mr Miller's bank. T
4 Mr Miller tells Marnie not to tell anyone about the false accounts. T
5 Mr Miller has got copies of the false accounts in his red book. T
6 Mr Miller is going to burn the red book. F
7 Marnie and Mr Miller are happy to see Hannah on the stairs. F
8 Graces pushes Hannah down the stairs. F

5 Answer the questions.

1 What does Mrs Frost say that she'll give to Marnie?

....

2 Who goes for walks with Hannah while Hannah is getting better?

....

3 When Hannah goes downstairs, what does she want to make?

....

4 Where did Marnie put the false accounts?

....

LOOKING FORWARD

6 What do you think? Answer the questions.

1 Why has Hannah fallen unconscious?

....

2 Chapter 3 is called *Alone*. Who will be alone? Why?

....

Chapter 3

Alone

'Oh, my head hurts,' whispered Hannah. There was a glass of water on the table beside her bed. She drank some, and after a few minutes, she began to feel better.

It was daytime, but the house was strangely quiet. She could hear people outside in the street. Some boys were shouting and somewhere a baby was crying.

'Marnie and Grace must be out,' she thought.

Her travelling clothes were on her chair. 'The *Titanic* sails today!' she said. 'I'm going to New York.'

She jumped out of bed, ran down the stairs and called Marnie and Grace. Nobody answered.

She looked around. Marnie's cases weren't by the door. There were no breakfast plates on the kitchen table. There was nothing on the sitting room table. The cases, the tickets, the money ... everything had gone. Hannah was alone.

'I expect Marnie and Grace are coming back for me,' she thought. 'I'll get ready.'

She went back upstairs and put on her travelling clothes. The large bag with her dresses was gone.

'They've taken it to the ship already,' she thought. She packed her nightdress and wash bag into her small bag. Then, as she put on her watch, she saw the time. It was eleven o'clock. The ship was sailing at twelve.

'Something's happened to Marnie. She can't get back here in time,' thought Hannah. 'But I can get to the ship if I hurry.' She picked up her bag, ran downstairs, locked the house and walked quickly along the street.

As she passed the bread shop, the shopkeeper called out, 'Miss Frost! You've come back!'

'Come back?' said Hannah, stopping to speak to him. 'I'm sorry, what do you mean?'

'Well, you left yesterday,' said the shopkeeper.

'Yesterday?' said Hannah. 'I don't understand.'

'Didn't you leave yesterday morning – on the ship?' asked the shopkeeper. 'With Marnie? I saw you go. You waved to me from the carriage – don't you remember?'

'Yes, of course,' said Hannah. But she didn't remember at all. 'I was unwell ... I must go. Goodbye!'

She continued down the street, trying to understand what the shopkeeper had said. As she turned a corner, she walked into a boy who was selling newspapers.

'Hey, watch where you're going!' he said. Hannah looked at the newspaper he was holding. In large letters on the front page, it said '*Titanic leaves for New York*'.

'I don't understand,' she said. She looked at the date of the newspaper: Thursday 11th April 1912.

'Isn't it Wednesday today?' she said to the boy.

'No, Miss,' said the boy. 'Today's Thursday.'

Hannah didn't speak.

'Are you all right, Miss?' the boy asked.

She walked slowly back to the house, went into her father's study and sat at his desk. She put her head in her hands as she began to understand.

'I saw Marnie with Mr Miller on Tuesday evening, and today is Thursday. So … I slept all day Wednesday and all of Wednesday night. I slept for thirty-six hours!' she thought. 'And Marnie has gone without me.'

And then things became clearer to Hannah. She had heard Marnie and Mr Miller talking … Grace had shouted behind her … their faces were angry … and then, nothing.

It was the hot chocolate, she realised. Marnie had put something in her hot chocolate.

Hannah's mother had said that Marnie was a part of the family. Well, that was wrong – Marnie was working for Mr Miller.

She tried to remember their conversation. Mr Miller had a book – a red book – and it showed that her father was innocent.

'Perhaps if I get that red book, I can take it to Father in New York,' thought Hannah. 'And if Marnie's right, it will show the world that he's not a thief[6]. But how can I get it?'

Then she had an idea. She ran up to her room and brought a pretty wooden box back downstairs. She opened her bag and found some earrings, a blue pocket mirror, some scarves and other pretty things, and she took off her watch. They were all presents from her mother, except for the watch. That was from her father, and it was very special to her. She put the things in the box. She closed her bag, picked up the box and went out.

Mr Miller had invited the Frost family to his house in Archers Road just once, three years before. It was much bigger than the Frosts' house in Bellevue Road. She remembered large rooms with pictures on all the walls and expensive furniture.

Half an hour later, Hannah was walking quickly along Archers Road. The Millers' house looked quiet – she hoped the family was out. She ran down the side steps and knocked at the servants'[7] door.

'Yes?' said a servant girl, opening the door.

'Excuse me,' said Hannah. 'I'm selling—'

'We don't buy from street sellers,' said the girl, starting to shut the door. 'The lady of the house doesn't like it.'

'Wait! Perhaps *you* are interested,' said Hannah. She held out the box. 'I'm selling things for young ladies like you. Pretty earrings. Scarves. My prices are low.'

The girl looked into the box. Her face lit up.

'Come in, then,' she said. 'Just for a few minutes. Everyone's out except me.'

They sat at the table in the kitchen.

'What's your name?' asked Hannah.

'Daisy,' said the girl. 'Here, have a biscuit. I've just made them.'

While Hannah ate her biscuit, Daisy started to talk.

'I'm only here for two more days, anyway,' said Daisy. 'Mr Miller's going to America and Mrs Miller's going to Scotland. I won't have a job after Saturday. I want to give myself a little present. And I like to look pretty for my young man. So let's see what you've got.'

Hannah took a blue flower from the box. She put it in Daisy's hair, using a hairpin to keep it in place. 'Oh, you look very pretty,' she said. 'Who's going to America, did you say?'

'Mr Miller,' said Daisy. 'He's just taking his man servant. His wife and daughters are going to Scotland. They don't need me. So it's, "Thanks very much, Daisy, and out you go into the street." I've worked for them for two years!'

'That's not fair!' said Hannah. 'I'm surprised Mr Miller didn't go on that new ship – the *Titanic*.'

'Ooh, yes, wasn't it lovely?' said Daisy. 'I ran down to watch it leave. Mr Miller wanted to go on it, but he had to go to London yesterday. He's going on a ship called the *An— An—* ... I can't remember. But I know it begins with "A"!'

'When is that ship sailing?' asked Hannah.

'On Saturday,' said Daisy. 'And that's when my job ends.'

'I expect he's going on business,' said Hannah, trying not to sound too interested.

'Yes, he's opening a new bank in America – Miller's Bank, New York!' said Daisy. 'And don't tell anyone, but I heard him talking to his wife. He wants to catch a criminal in New York too – a thief called Henry Frost.'

'Oh!' said Hannah. 'I ... yes, I think I read about him.'

'Well, he worked at Miller's Bank,' Daisy said. 'I saw him here lots of times. But then he took people's money out of the bank for himself! Can you believe it? And it wasn't rich people's money – it belonged to ordinary people, like shopkeepers and office workers. Terrible! Mr Miller thinks Mr Frost should be in prison.' Hannah felt sick as she listened to Daisy. Her dear, kind father! Everyone thought he was a thief.

Hannah had come to this house to try and get the red book. Now she knew she *must* get it.

'Well, Daisy,' she said, 'will you buy anything?'

'I'd like this little mirror,' she said. 'How much is it?'

'Er ... six pence,' said Hannah quickly.

'All right, I'll just go and get my purse. My room's at the top of the house. You wait here. Don't touch anything.'

Daisy left the kitchen. Hannah stood up. 'It's now or never,' she thought. She walked up the servants' stairs to the main part of the house, listening carefully. Daisy would soon come downstairs, and the Millers might come back at any time.

She found Mr Miller's study. There were books all around the walls. And then she saw what she was looking for. On a large desk was a red book with gold numbers on the front.

Chapter 4

A bowl of soup

'Yes!' thought Hannah, as she ran towards the book on Mr Miller's desk. But then she looked at it more closely. 'No!' she said.

It was a red book, but it was the wrong one. The date in gold wasn't 1911 – it was 1912. She looked around the room. Behind the desk was a shelf full of red books. She pulled out two of them. One was 1902, the other was 1909. Hannah quickly pushed the 1902 book back into the shelf. She hid the 1909 book in her dress pocket under her coat.

'It might be useful,' she thought, and then she ran.

Hannah sat down quickly at the kitchen table. A few moments later, Daisy came back. At the same time, a bell rang on the kitchen wall.

'Oh, Mrs Miller and the girls are back,' said Daisy. 'Quick – I'll buy the mirror. Do you want to show the other things to Mrs Miller? You're not like the other street sellers round here. Her girls might like something.'

'No,' said Hannah. 'I've got to go now.'

'Oh, I've only got five pence,' said Daisy, looking in her purse.

'That's fine, Daisy. I'll take five pence,' said Hannah. 'And keep the flower too.'

When Hannah got back to Bellevue Road, a man was standing at the front door of her house.

'Hello?' she said. 'Can I help you?'

'I don't think so,' said the man. 'I'm the rent man. I'm just locking the house. The family here has gone.'

'What? But that's *my* family. I live here,' said Hannah. 'I'm sure my mother paid the rent until the end of this week.'

'That's not what it says here,' he said, holding up a black notebook. 'A new family is moving in tomorrow.'

'Oh! Can I stay here just for tonight?' she said.

'No,' said the man.

'Well, can I get my things? My bag is in there. It's in the study,' she said.

'Wait here,' said the man.

A few moments later he returned with Hannah's bag, and handed it to her. Then he locked the front door again and walked away. The conversation was finished.

Hannah put the wooden box into the bag. Then she went to the house next door. The Bunney family lived there. She and Lizzie Bunney had been in the same class at school when they were little. She knocked on the door.

Mrs Bunney opened it. She saw Hannah and said, 'Oh, it's you. I have nothing to say to you or your family.'

'Mrs Bunney,' called Hannah, as the door shut in her face. 'Please! I need help.' But the door stayed shut.

Hannah went to Dr Mason's. He would help her. But his door was locked. A note in the window said 'Closed for one month'. Hannah remembered that he was away in Liverpool.

She went to the bread shop. The shopkeeper had spoken to her that morning. He wasn't there now, but his wife was.

'Yes?' she said, not smiling.

'I need help,' Hannah started. 'I—'

'I'm not helping you,' the woman said. Her voice got louder. 'My husband thinks your father is innocent, but I don't agree. Go away.'

Hannah walked out of the shop. She wanted to cry. The world was against her.

She went into a park and sat down. Children were playing games on the grass. She watched them, and she felt terribly lonely. Her family was on the other side of the Atlantic Ocean.

As Hannah sat there, alone, she became angry with her father. He was safe in New York. People weren't shouting at him. They were shouting at her. But then she remembered his kind face and his honest eyes. She remembered his last words to her, on the night he left for America.

'If I don't go, Hannah, they'll put me in prison,' he had explained. 'Mr Miller has too many important friends. Nobody will believe that I'm innocent.'

The sun began to go down and Hannah felt cold.

'Where can I sleep tonight?' she thought. She picked up her things and walked towards the town centre.

Two women were giving out bowls of hot soup in a room beside a church. People in dirty clothes were waiting quietly. Although some of the people smelled horrible, Hannah was hungry and she joined them.

When it was Hannah's turn, the women looked at her clothes.

'This meal is for poor people,' one of them said.

'Please,' said Hannah. 'I haven't eaten today. I've only got five pence in my purse and I'm alone in the world. May I have a bowl of soup?'

The woman looked at Hannah. 'All right,' she said. 'I don't know if I believe you, but you look hungry.'

Hannah sat down at a long table next to an old woman. The soup didn't taste good, but it was warm. The old woman drank her soup noisily.

'What are you doing here?' asked the woman.

'I've lost my parents,' said Hannah. 'They've gone to America.'

'What are you going to do?'

'There's a ship sailing to New York on Saturday. I'm going to be on it.'

The woman laughed. 'You need money for that. Or are you getting on the ship without paying?'

'I don't know,' said Hannah. 'But I'll be on that ship.'

LOOKING BACK

1. Check your answers to *Looking forward* on page 17.

ACTIVITIES

2. Match the times with the events.

   1 Tuesday evening [e]
   2 Wednesday morning [ ]
   3 Wednesday midday [ ]
   4 Thursday morning [ ]
   5 Thursday just after 11 am [ ]

   a Hannah wakes up with a headache.
   b The shopkeeper sees Marnie and a young woman leave.
   c Hannah talks to the newspaper boy.
   d The *Titanic* sails.
   ~~e~~ Hannah drinks the hot chocolate and falls unconscious.

3. Tick (✓) the things that Hannah learns from Daisy.

   1 Mr Miller is going to America. [✓]
   2 He's taking his daughters with him. [ ]
   3 He didn't go on the *Titanic* because there were no tickets left. [ ]
   4 He's travelling on a ship that sails on Saturday. [ ]
   5 He's going on a holiday. [ ]
   6 He's opening a new bank in New York. [ ]
   7 He's sailing back to Southampton the next day. [ ]
   8 He wants to find Hannah's father in New York. [ ]

4 Tick (✓) the correct answers.

1 Hannah sees a red book on Mr Miller's desk. What is the year on it?

1902 ☐ 1909 ☐ 1911 ☐ 1912 ☑

2 Hannah puts a red book in her dress pocket. What is the year on it?

1902 ☐ 1909 ☐ 1911 ☐ 1912 ☒

3 What does Daisy buy from Hannah?

a purse ☐ a mirror ☐ a hairpin ☒

4 Who helps Hannah after her visit to Mr Miller's house?

Mrs Bunney ☒ Dr Mason ☐

a woman at the church ☐

5 Answer the questions.

1 Who does the shopkeeper think he saw leaving with Marnie?

....

2 Who did the shopkeeper really see leaving with Marnie?

....

3 What does Hannah want to get when she goes to Mr Miller's house?

....

4 Why does Hannah feel sick when Daisy starts talking about her father?

....

LOOKING FORWARD

6 Tick (✓) what you think happens in the next two chapters.

1 Hannah sleeps the night in a park. ☐

2 Hannah gets help from the police. ☐

3 Hannah gets enough money for a ticket to America. ☐

Chapter 5

Seven hours

It was early evening when Hannah went into the Central Library. The library assistants were busy at the front desk, and Hannah quickly walked past. She sat in a quiet corner.

At five minutes to seven, a bell rang. The library was closing. She heard one of the assistants walking between the shelves. As the assistant passed by, Hannah quickly moved to the other side of a shelf. When the assistant returned, she moved the other way.

'Everyone's gone,' the assistant called to the front desk. Hannah could hear the assistants joking together as they put on their coats. They were lucky, she thought. They had warm homes to go to. A few minutes later, they turned out all the lights and locked up. Hannah spent an uncomfortable night on a long wooden seat, using her coat as a blanket.

* * *

The sound of a key in the main door woke Hannah. Morning light was coming through the window. She put on her coat and hat. The clock on the wall said seven, and the library didn't open until nine thirty. She hid and watched.

Two men started to wash the windows. Hannah stayed behind the shelves and moved quietly towards the main door. As she opened the door, one of the men called, 'Hello!'

Hannah turned round. 'Oh,' she said. 'Are you open?'

'Open? It's seven o'clock in the morning!' said the man, laughing. 'It's too early for reading.'

'Wait a minute! Were you in here all night?' asked the other man.

'No, of course not! I'll come back later,' Hannah said, and left quickly.

She walked down to the docks[8]. A very large passenger ship was waiting there. Its name was on the side, in white letters: *Andromeda*. Daisy had said the name of Mr Miller's ship began with an 'A'. So this was it.

A few people were waiting for the ticket office to open and Hannah joined them. More people arrived and stood behind her – a poor family with lots of children, an older couple and a tall young man. At nine o'clock, the office opened, and they all went in.

'How much is a third class ticket to New York on the *Andromeda*?' Hannah asked the man at the desk.

'Three pounds,' said the man. 'That's to share a cabin[9] with one other person.'

'When do you stop selling tickets?' asked Hannah.

'Five o'clock this evening. That's when we make the list[10] of passengers. The *Andromeda* sails at midday tomorrow,' said the man.

Outside the office, Hannah looked in her purse. There was Daisy's five pence.

'I'll need three pounds for the ticket and some more money for food on the journey. That's a lot,' she said to herself. 'And I've got seven hours to get it.'

Hannah walked quickly to the railway station. She went into the Ladies' room, washed her face, and brushed her hair and teeth. Then she had breakfast in the station café.

Back in the centre of town, she found a silver shop. She walked up and down outside for a few minutes. Selling to Daisy had been easy, but she felt nervous about selling in a shop.

'Come on, Hannah, you have to do this,' she said to herself, and she went in.

'I'd like to sell these,' she said, showing the shopkeeper a ring, two pairs of earrings and her silver watch. 'How much can you give me for them?'

As the shopkeeper looked at Hannah's hat, coat and shoes, she felt her face go red. She wanted to run out of the door.

'You don't look like a thief,' he said. 'Are they yours?'

'They were birthday presents,' said Hannah. 'But I'm going to America, and I'd like to sell them.'

'Well, Miss,' said the shopkeeper. 'I can't give you much. Nobody's buying silver at the moment. How about one pound?'

‘Thank you,’ said Hannah, picking up her things, ‘but I’ll take them to another shop. I know that my father paid over a pound for the watch alone.’

‘I’m sorry,’ said the shopkeeper. ‘That’s my final offer.’

‘I think they’re worth more,’ said Hannah. She went to the door.

‘All right,’ called the shopkeeper. ‘Will you take two pounds?’

‘Yes,’ said Hannah, coming back. ‘Thank you.’

At a little shop near the docks, Hannah sold two rings, some scarves and the wooden box. She got a very good price for the box, and by the middle of the afternoon, she had nearly four pounds in her purse. She felt pleased with her day’s work and stopped for a cup of tea and a cake in a restaurant. She hadn’t eaten since breakfast and was very tired. The clock on the wall said four o’clock. There was lots of time. She sat in a warm, dark corner and her eyes began to close.

‘Miss!’ said the waitress, shaking Hannah’s arm. ‘Miss! You’re asleep.’

‘Oh!’ said Hannah, waking suddenly. ‘What time is it?’

‘It’s quarter to five,’ said the waitress. ‘Here’s your bill.’

Hannah quickly paid the waitress, and ran. Ten minutes later, she arrived at the ticket office. It was still open.

‘One third class ticket for the *Andromeda*, please,’ she said to the man behind the desk.

‘Sorry, Miss,’ said the man. ‘You’re too late.’

‘It’s two minutes to five,’ she said. ‘Look at the clock!’

‘The time isn’t the problem,’ said the man. ‘There aren’t any tickets left. We’ve sold out.’

Chapter 6

Goodbye, England

'No tickets? I don't believe it!' said Hannah. 'What about in second class?'

'I'm sorry, Miss,' said the man behind the ticket desk. 'The ship's completely full.'

There was a chair in the office and Hannah threw herself into it. She put her head in her hands. Then the man called her back to the desk.

'I've just remembered something. Wait there,' he said, and went into the back office. He returned with an envelope. 'What's your name, Miss?' he asked.

'Frost, Hannah Frost,' she said.

'Well, Miss Frost, you're in luck,' he said, holding out the envelope.

Hannah took it. Her name was written on the front, and inside there was a ticket – a third class ticket for the *Andromeda*.

'Oh!' said Hannah. 'Where did this come from?'

'A young man bought the ticket this morning. He asked for an envelope and left it with me. He told me to give it to you,' said the man.

'I don't understand,' said Hannah. 'Who was he?'

'I don't know, Miss. He told me your name and said you were alone, but he didn't tell me *his* name.'

'But … what did he look like?' asked Hannah.

'He was just a young man,' he said. 'It was early this morning and the office was busy. I didn't look at him closely. I think he was wearing a grey suit and he was tall. Now, if you'll excuse me, we need to make the passenger list.'

Hannah went outside, ticket in hand. She didn't know what to think. She knew she must go on the *Andromeda*. It was her only chance to get the red book, and she wanted to get to her parents. But who was this young man in a grey suit? Was he a friend or not? And why had he bought her a ticket?

Hannah knew a small hotel near the railway station. She got a clean little room there for just a few pennies. It was a noisy part of town, but Hannah was tired after her uncomfortable night in the library. She fell asleep at once.

* * *

Hannah woke early and was at the docks by seven o'clock, five hours before the *Andromeda* was going to sail. There was a lot of activity. Men were carrying cases and bags, boxes of fruit and vegetables, big pieces of meat and bags of letters onto the ship. Passengers were arriving by carriage and car.

A ship's officer was checking passengers' tickets. He found Hannah's name on his passenger list.

'Welcome to the *Andromeda*, Miss Frost,' he said.

Hannah went straight to her cabin in third class. There were two beds, and two young women already sitting on one of them.

'Hello,' she said. 'I think I'm in this cabin. My name's Hannah.'

'Nice to meet you,' said one of the girls. 'I'm Edith and this is my sister, Roberta. I'm just visiting Roberta. We couldn't get a cabin together. My cabin is on the next deck[11] down.'

'Who are you sharing with?' Hannah asked Edith.

'An old lady – her name's Mrs Easton,' said Edith.

Hannah couldn't believe her luck. 'Would you like to change cabins with me, Edith?' she offered. 'I don't mind which cabin I'm in.'

'Really?' said Edith. 'We'd love that.'

'Let's go, then,' said Hannah.

Hannah followed the girls down to her new cabin on the next deck. Mrs Easton was unpacking her case. The sisters introduced Hannah to her and she was very friendly.

'Just one thing,' Hannah said to the sisters as they were leaving. 'A young man may come to the cabin and ask for me. Don't tell him anything. Say that you've never heard of me. Is that all right?'

'Yes, of course!' said Roberta. 'How exciting!'

It was still only nine o'clock. Hannah unpacked some of her things, hiding the red book from Mr Miller's study at the bottom of her bag. Then she started to look around the ship. She went confidently up the stairs to one of the first class decks. The first class decks were for first class passengers only, but her travelling clothes were the latest fashion, and she looked like a first class passenger.

Some of the first class cabins opened onto a wide deck with glass walls along the side of the ship. Here the passengers could sit and watch the sea without getting cold or wet. These were the largest cabins, each with its own sitting room, as well as a bedroom and bathroom.

Many of the cabins were still empty, and Hannah looked into one.

'Are you lost, Miss?' asked an officer, as he walked by.

'No, I'm just looking for my mother,' she said. 'Perhaps she's gone down to the dining room. I'll look there. Bye!' and she walked quickly to the nearest stairs.

Later, she found the telegraph room. A radio officer was working there. Hannah went in.

'Good morning, Miss,' said the officer.

'Hello,' said Hannah, smiling. 'What happens in here?'

'I use this machine to send and receive messages,' he said.

Hannah saw a list of names on the officer's desk. He was resting his arm on it. It was the ship's passenger list. She could see the cabin numbers beside each name, and she wanted a closer look.

'Can I bring my friends up later – to show them the machine?' she asked the officer.

'Yes, Miss.'

'Thank you,' said Hannah.

After touring the dining rooms, the swimming pool and the library, Hannah climbed up to the top deck. Three loud bells sounded through the ship – the *Andromeda* was sailing in ten minutes' time. Hannah stayed on the top deck to say goodbye to England. She watched the last few passengers coming onto the ship.

Then a car came very fast along the dock. It was Mr Miller. Hannah watched as he and a servant got out of the car and came onto the *Andromeda*. Two of the ship's men followed, carrying Mr Miller's large travelling case.

'Is the red book in there?' thought Hannah.

The *Andromeda* slowly sailed out of Southampton and began its great journey across the ocean.

* * *

Hannah went to visit the sisters. She offered to take them on a tour of the ship. When they got to the telegraph office, the sisters were very excited.

'Can we send a message to our grandparents?' asked Edith.

'We're going to visit them in Washington,' said Roberta.

The passenger list was now on the table. While the telegraph officer was sending the sisters' message, with his back to the table, Hannah quickly looked at the list. There were hundreds of names, but under 'First Class', she saw Mr Miller's name and his cabin number – Deck A, Cabin 7.

Suddenly her plan felt real. She had to get into Cabin 7 on Deck A – but how?

LOOKING BACK

1 Check your answers to *Looking forward* on page 29.

ACTIVITIES

2 Put the numbers in the correct sentences.

two	two	~~three~~	four	five	forty-five

1 A third class ticket on the *Andromeda* costs ...three... pounds.

2 The ticket office will stop selling tickets on the *Andromeda* at .... o'clock.

3 The shopkeeper gives Hannah .... pounds for her silver.

4 Hannah makes nearly .... pounds by selling her things.

5 Hannah falls asleep for .... minutes in the warm little restaurant.

6 She arrives at the ticket office .... minutes before it closes.

3 Underline the correct words in each sentence.

1 Hannah is too late to buy a ticket because *the ship is full* / *the office has closed*.

2 Hannah *knows* / *doesn't know* the young man who has bought her ticket.

3 The night before the ship sails, Hannah sleeps *in the library* / *in a hotel*.

4 Edith changes cabins with *Mrs Easton* / *Hannah*.

5 Hannah *is* / *looks like* a first class passenger.

6 Hannah goes back to the telegraph office because she wants to *look at the passenger list* / *send a message*.

4 Put the sentences in order.

1 Hannah goes up to the top deck and sees Mr Miller arrive. ☐
2 The sisters take Hannah to meet Mrs Easton. ☐
3 Hannah goes up to look at one of the first class decks. ☐
4 Hannah takes the sisters to the telegraph room. ☐
5 Hannah meets Edith and Roberta. [1]
6 Hannah meets a radio officer in the telegraph room. ☐
7 Hannah sees Mr Miller's name and cabin number. ☐

5 Match the two parts of the sentences.

1 Hannah thinks the library assistants are lucky because [b]
2 Hannah decides to sell her things so that ☐
3 Hannah walks up and down outside the silver shop because ☐
4 Hannah wants to change cabins with Edith so that ☐
5 Hannah wants to find out Mr Miller's cabin number so that ☐

a the tall young man won't find her.
~~b~~ they have warm homes to go to.
c she can search for the red book there.
d she feels nervous.
e she'll have enough money for a ticket on the *Andromeda*.

LOOKING FORWARD

6 Tick (✓) what you think happens in the next three chapters.

1 Hannah is brave enough to go into Mr Miller's cabin. ☐
2 Mr Miller speaks to Hannah. ☐
3 Hannah meets the young man who bought her ticket. ☐

Chapter 7

Nowhere to hide

The *Andromeda* sailed quietly through the black waters of the ocean during the night. It would soon reach the ice fields of the Atlantic, with their great icebergs.

Early in the morning, Hannah lay awake, thinking. Had Mr Miller known that Marnie planned to leave her at home? Had he expected Hannah to take the next ship – the *Andromeda*? Perhaps he was hoping to follow Hannah. She knew he wanted to find her father – Daisy had told her that.

At breakfast time, Hannah went into the dining room. The sisters ran over to her table.

'That young man came to ask for you last night,' Edith said. 'We didn't let him in – we were already in bed!'

'What did he look like?' asked Hannah.

'He was very handsome,' said Roberta. 'Tall, blond hair, grey eyes, grey suit.'

'What did he say?' asked Hannah.

'He said, "I'm looking for a Miss Frost. I thought this was her cabin,"' said Edith.

'And we said, "We've never heard of a Miss Frost. This is our cabin and our name is not Miss Frost!"' said Roberta.

The sisters laughed loudly at this.

The next morning Hannah found a quiet corner on the top deck, and spent the day there. The Atlantic air was cold but wonderful, and the sun was shining. She thought through her plan several times. That evening she would try to get into Mr Miller's cabin when he was at dinner, and look for the red book. She would put the 1909 red book in its place.

She wasn't confident. Would she find the book? Had Mr Miller brought it with him? She didn't know. But she had to try.

When the sun went down, Hannah went back to her cabin. She put the 1909 red book in her dress pocket.

Just after seven o'clock, Hannah went to the stairs that led to Deck A. Mr Miller's cabin was up there. She waited for a few minutes, looking at a dinner menu on the wall. The next half hour could go badly wrong and she was very nervous. When a family with noisy children came by, she followed them up to Deck A. She walked past the cabin doors, checking the numbers until she found number 7. She continued slowly past it. Passengers were going in and out of their cabins all along the deck, getting ready for dinner.

The *Andromeda* was just sailing into the first ice field.

'Look!' shouted a passenger. 'An iceberg!'

Cabin doors opened as other passengers went to look. Mr Miller and his servant came out. They joined the crowd of people looking at the iceberg.

This was Hannah's chance – it was now or never. 'Be brave, Hannah,' she whispered to herself, and walked into Mr Miller's cabin. Nobody saw her.

Inside, she looked around quickly. There was a large sitting room with chairs, a desk and a wardrobe, and a smaller bedroom with a bathroom. She needed somewhere to hide before they came back.

The wardrobe door was open and inside was a long black coat. She got in behind the coat and stood still. Her mouth was dry and her body was shaking. She had never been so afraid.

'I hope the captain[12] has seen that iceberg,' the servant was saying as he and Mr Miller came back into the cabin. 'There are probably others ahead.'

Hannah watched from the wardrobe.

'These ships sail across the Atlantic every week,' said Mr Miller. 'They always go through these ice fields. Don't worry – the captain knows all about them.'

'Shall I come back after dinner, sir?' asked the servant.

'No, I won't need you again this evening,' said Mr Miller. 'I'm just going to look at a few papers, and then I'm joining the captain for dinner. You can go now.'

'Thank you, sir,' said the servant, and then he left the cabin.

Mr Miller opened his big travelling case. It opened like a book, into two halves. Hannah could see right into it from her hiding place. On one side were hats and shoes. On the other side were drawers. Mr Miller opened a drawer and pulled out some papers. He took them to the desk.

And there, in the same drawer, Hannah could see something red. Was it the book?

Mr Miller made some notes and then put the papers back.

He locked the travelling case, and then walked straight towards the wardrobe. Hannah nearly cried out. Mr Miller put the key into a coat pocket and closed the wardrobe door.

Hannah heard the cabin door close, and slowly opened the wardrobe door. She found the key in the coat pocket, unlocked the travelling case and opened the drawer. There was the red book. On the front was the date '1911'. This was it!

She took the 1909 book from her pocket. The two books looked the same, except for the date. She put the 1911 book in her pocket and put the 1909 book into the drawer. She turned it over so the date on the front didn't show.

Hannah closed the case and returned the key. Then she went to the cabin door and tried to open it. But it was locked. She hadn't thought of that. Suddenly, there was a noise. Someone was opening the door. There was no time to hide.

'Oh!' cried Hannah, jumping back from the door.

There was the tall young man in the grey suit.

Chapter 8

Leo Zimmerman

'I don't want to alarm you, Miss Frost,' said the young man. 'But it isn't very safe for you to be in here.'

'N-no,' said Hannah. 'How did you open the door? Have you got a key?'

The young man smiled and held up a hairpin.

'Why would I need a key?' he said. 'Come out and I'll lock it again.'

Hannah came out of the cabin. She was shaking. The young man put the hairpin in the lock and moved it around.

'There – it's locked again,' he said. 'Now, let's go. We don't want anyone to see us up here.'

The young man walked quickly along the deck and Hannah followed him. 'Who are you?' she asked.

But he replied, 'Are you hungry? We could have dinner in the dining room on my deck. I'm in second class.'

'Are you working for Mr Miller?' asked Hannah.

'No,' he laughed. 'No. Please relax – I'm a friend.'

Hannah didn't smile, and she didn't relax.

In the dining room, a waiter showed them to a table. The young man sat opposite Hannah. She looked closely at his face for the first time.

'Don't I know you?' said Hannah.

'Yes, I'm sorry. Let me introduce myself,' said the young man. 'My name's Leo ... Leo Zimmerman.'

'Leo Zimmerman,' repeated Hannah. 'You work at Mr Miller's bank, don't you?'

'I *used* to work there,' said Leo. 'I've seen you at the bank a few times.'

'I remember my father talking about you,' said Hannah. 'He liked you. But *are* you working for Mr Miller?'

'No,' said Leo. 'I'm working for your father.'

'What?' said Hannah. The people at the next table looked at her. 'My father?' she whispered. 'Do you know where he is?'

'No,' said Leo. 'I haven't heard from him since he went to America. Don't *you* know where he is?'

'No,' she said. She sat unhappily back in her chair. 'What's happening, Leo? Why are you here?'

'Let me start at the beginning,' said Leo. 'I used to work closely with your father at the bank. When he realised that the police were coming for him, he decided to escape to

America. He knew that Mr Miller had important friends in England. And he knew that he would never get a fair trial[13] in Southampton.'

'Yes, that's what he said to me,' said Hannah.

'He sent me some money. He asked me to meet him at Southampton docks. I bought him a ticket for a ship to America, using a false name. He went onto the ship in the dark. There were police posters of him at the docks, but he had cut his hair and beard. He looked like a different man. He asked me to use the rest of the money to help his family and to watch Mr Miller. I promised him that I would help you. Your father is innocent.'

The waiter brought their food, and Leo stopped speaking.

Hannah waited for the waiter to leave. Then she asked, 'How did you know I needed a ticket?'

'I spoke to your mother before she left for America. She told me that you were sailing on the *Titanic* with your family servant.'

'Yes,' said Hannah. 'That was the plan. But Marnie – our servant – took her daughter in my place.'

'I went down to the docks the day the *Titanic* sailed – I saw them leave. Then, the next day, I went to your house to look for you. You weren't there and the house was locked up. I didn't know how to find you.'

'The rent man locked me out!' said Hannah.

'So I tried to think what you would do next. And that's when I bought you a ticket for the *Andromeda*.'

'But why are you on this ship?' asked Hannah.

'I lost my job at the bank after all the trouble. I tried to get another job, but nobody was interested – because I had worked with your ...' Leo didn't finish his sentence.

'Of course,' said Hannah, 'I understand.'

'So I decided to make a new life in America too. After you're safely with your family, I'm planning to look for work in New York.'

'Well, Leo Zimmerman,' said Hannah, smiling at last. 'You are brilliant. Thank you.'

They had finished their meal by now, and decided to go out on deck. The *Andromeda* was sailing quietly through the ice fields, between the icebergs.

Hannah was tired. She still had a hundred questions for Leo, but they could wait until tomorrow. She had one big question for herself. Was Leo telling the truth?

'I'll walk down to your cabin with you,' said Leo.

'No, that's not necessary,' said Hannah. 'Thank you for everything, Leo. Goodnight.'

And she went down to the third class deck alone, checking that no one was following her.

* * *

The next morning Hannah and Leo met for breakfast.

'Tell me about the trouble at the bank,' said Hannah. 'You were there. You must know what happened.'

'Yes, it was all Mr Miller's idea. He offered very high interest rates[14] to some of his customers. He said he was putting their money into some amazing business in China. There was no amazing business, of course. But a lot of people trusted[15] him and gave him their money.'

'How was he able to pay the high interest rates to his customers?' Hannah asked.

'He was using money from new customers to pay the old ones,' Leo explained.

'That's dishonest,' said Hannah.

'Yes, of course it is,' said Leo. 'And when some of the customers found out, Mr Miller blamed your father.'

'And Marnie helped him! I heard her tell Mr Miller. Father often brought his important papers home to work on. She took Father's real accounts from his desk and put Mr Miller's false accounts in their place.'

Hannah told Leo about the hot chocolate and the empty house. She didn't say anything about her visit to Mr Miller's house. Could she trust him? She didn't know.

'How are we going to find your parents?' asked Leo.

'I don't know,' replied Hannah. 'My mother's expecting me to arrive on the *Titanic*. But I won't be on it, and she won't know why. She won't know I'm on this ship.'

'Where did you agree to meet her?' asked Leo.

'At the White Star office.'

'Why don't you send a message there?' he said. 'She'll get it when she goes to meet you.'

'Yes, of course,' said Hannah. 'I'll do that right away. My message needs to reach New York before the *Titanic*.'

There was a crowd of passengers in the telegraph office. Some of them seemed quite angry. Hannah and Leo tried to see what was happening. The telegraph officer stood up.

'Please, please, ladies and gentlemen[16],' he said. 'I can't send your telegrams today.'

'But I must send this message,' shouted a man. 'It's very important.'

'Let the officer speak,' said another man.

The captain arrived and the room became quiet.

'Ladies and gentlemen,' said the captain. 'I have some bad news. Our telegraph machine is not working. We are not able to send or receive any messages. When we are able to mend it, I will tell you. Please be patient. There's nothing the telegraph officer can do. Thank you.'

Hannah was trying not to cry. 'How am I going to find my family now?' she thought.

Chapter 9

In the mirror

Later that morning, Hannah took Leo up to her quiet corner on the top deck. They sat and looked out at the sea. There were clouds in the sky and there was a cold wind. Hannah pulled her coat close around her.

'What were you looking for in Mr Miller's cabin, by the way?' asked Leo.

'I was looking for something to help my father,' said Hannah.

'Did you find anything?' Leo asked.

Hannah had already decided not to tell him about the book. 'No,' she said. 'Nothing.'

'Perhaps we should go back to his cabin for a second look.'

'Oh no! I couldn't do that again,' said Hannah.

It started to rain. They went inside and said goodbye, agreeing to meet for lunch. Hannah borrowed a book from the ship's library and went to the third class lounge. She opened the book, but she kept reading the same sentence over and over again. She just didn't feel like reading.

There was a little shop on her deck. It sold postcards, hats, sweets and other things. Hannah went to have a look in it.

She didn't see anything interesting there, so she went up to the shop on the second class deck. It had more things. She asked to see some earrings.

'Do they go with my dress?' she asked the assistant.

'Oh, yes. Have a look,' said the assistant, holding up a large mirror. Hannah turned her head a little to look at the earrings. Suddenly, behind her, she saw Leo in the mirror. He was standing outside the shop, talking to someone. She held the mirror and looked more closely. Leo was talking to Mr Miller.

'Are you all right, Miss?' asked the shop assistant. 'You've gone white. Would you like to sit down?'

'I'm … Yes, I will sit down. Thank you,' said Hannah.

She sat down, away from the shop window, and waited until the men had gone.

Hannah stayed in her cabin for the rest of the day. She didn't meet Leo for lunch. They had sailed into a storm, and the ship was moving slowly from side to side. The old lady in her cabin, Mrs Easton, was sick three times. Hannah felt bad too, but not because of the storm. She wasn't seasick. It was Leo.

'I'll never trust anyone again,' she thought.

* * *

The next morning the storm had passed and the ship travelled quietly through the water. Hannah helped Mrs Easton out onto the deck for some air. She found her a chair to sit on and got her a cup of tea. All the decks were crowded. Some of the passengers looked very white and unwell.

Back in her cabin, alone, Hannah took out Mr Miller's red book. She studied it closely. There were lists of names and addresses. She saw that some people had put in thousands of pounds. Most of the addresses were in Southampton and London. Some were in New York. Mr Miller had stolen money from customers on both sides of the Atlantic, and now he was opening a new bank in New York. So her father could be a problem for Mr Miller in America, as well as in England. Mr Frost knew too much, and Mr Miller wanted to shut him up. Hannah realised that her father was in real danger.

There was a knock on the door. Hannah quickly put the red book under the blanket and answered the door.

'Hello,' sang the sisters. Hannah relaxed.

'What a horrible night!' said Edith.

'Oh dear,' said Hannah. 'Were you very seasick?'

'We thought we were going to die,' said Roberta.

They came into Hannah's cabin and sat one on each side of her. They wanted to tell her about the handsome young man in the grey suit.

'He sat at our breakfast table,' said Edith.

'He asked about you,' said Roberta. 'He said you were friends now.'

'Did you tell him my cabin number?' asked Hannah.

'No, of course not,' said Roberta.

'We said we'd never heard of you,' said Edith.

'And we've come straight to tell you,' said Roberta.

They ran off, pleased with themselves. But when Hannah came out of her cabin, she was not surprised to see Leo. He was standing at the bottom of the stairs that came down to the deck. She locked her cabin and went to talk to him.

'Why didn't you come to lunch yesterday?' asked Leo.

'I wasn't feeling well,' said Hannah. 'The storm ...'

'Are you better now?' asked Leo, smiling.

'I'm fine,' said Hannah, turning away. 'I'm going back to my cabin now.'

'Is something wrong?' asked Leo. 'Why don't you want to talk to me?'

'I saw you yesterday,' said Hannah. 'I was in the shop.'

'What was I doing?' asked Leo. He stopped smiling.

'You were talking to Mr Miller,' said Hannah.

'Oh, yes,' said Leo, relaxing. 'That's what I've come to tell you. I met him on deck – you're right, just outside a shop. So you were watching, were you? I hope you don't think I'm working for him!'

'Yes, Leo, that *is* what I think,' said Hannah. 'You were talking to him – like a friend.'

'No, he just knows my face from the bank,' said Leo. 'He's never spoken to me before, but he saw me and said hello. He asked me why I was going to America. He wasn't really interested. He didn't even know I had left the bank.'

'What did you tell him?' asked Hannah.

‘I told him I was going to start a new life,’ explained Leo. ‘And that’s all.’

Now Hannah didn’t know what to think.

‘Come on, we were good friends yesterday,’ said Leo. ‘Let’s go and enjoy the sun.’

* * *

For the next few days the *Andromeda* sailed quietly on towards New York. Leo and Hannah spent most of the time together. He was very kind to her, and made her laugh. She began to trust him again.

On the tenth day of the journey, as Hannah and Leo were sitting in the lounge, there was an excited shout from outside. They ran out to see what it was.

‘Look at that!’ said Hannah.

It was the Statue of Liberty.

Ten minutes later, the captain called the passengers together in one of the large dining rooms.

'What's happening?' people asked as they crowded in. 'Why does he want to talk to us?'

Not all the passengers could get into the room. Many stood outside, trying to hear. Hannah and Leo were just inside the door. Hannah saw Mr Miller across the room, and hid behind Leo.

'Ladies and gentlemen,' said the captain. 'As you can see, we have arrived in New York.'

He told the passengers that the ship was at Ellis Island, across the river from the city. United States immigration[17] officers would soon come onto the ship with immigration forms for the first and second class passengers. Those passengers could then enter the United States. Third class passengers had to wait in the Immigration Station on Ellis Island. Immigration officers would talk to them there.

Then he said, 'But I have called you in here because I have some very sad news. Late last Sunday, on 14th April, the White Star's great new ship, the *Titanic*, hit an iceberg.'

Everyone started to talk at once.

'Quiet, please!' said the captain. Then he continued, 'The ship went down in the Atlantic in the early hours of Monday morning, just two days away from New York. Many lives were saved, but I am sad to say that many were lost.'

'No!' people called out around the room.

'My son!' one woman cried, and fell into her husband's arms, unconscious.

'Marnie and Grace!' whispered Hannah, and Leo put his arm around her.

LOOKING BACK

1 Check your answers to *Looking forward* on page 43.

ACTIVITIES

2 Put the sentences in order.

1 A passenger sees an iceberg. ☐
2 Hannah goes into the cabin and hides in the wardrobe. ☐
3 Hannah takes the 1911 book out of the travelling case. ☐
4 Mr Miller and his servant return to the cabin. ☐
5 Hannah goes up to Deck A. ☐
6 Hannah puts the 1909 book in her dress pocket. ☐
7 The servant leaves and then Mr Miller goes to dinner. ☐
8 Mr Miller and his servant come out of Cabin 7 to look at the iceberg. ☐

3 Underline the correct words in each sentence.

1 Edith and Roberta tell the young man that they *know / have never heard of* a Miss Frost.
2 The young man uses a *key / hairpin* to open the cabin door.
3 Hannah *has / hasn't* heard the name Leo Zimmerman before.
4 Mr Miller said he was putting his customers' money into a business in *America / China*.
5 Mr Miller used money from *China / new customers* to pay his old customers.
6 Hannah *can / can't* send a message to her mother.
7 The *captain / radio officer* tells the passengers the bad news about the *Titanic*.

4 Tick (✓) the things that Leo tells Hannah.

1 He is travelling in first class. ☐
2 He used to work at Mr Miller's bank. ☑
3 He is now working for Mr Frost, Hannah's father. ☐
4 He knows where Mr Frost is. ☐
5 He helped Mr Frost get away to America. ☐
6 Mr Frost used a false name and changed his appearance. ☐
7 Leo promised Mr Frost that he would help Hannah. ☐
8 Leo spoke to Mrs Frost before she left. ☐
9 Leo wants to go back to England as soon as he can. ☐
10 The trouble at the bank was all because of Mr Frost. ☐

5 Are the sentences true (*T*) or false (*F*)?

1 Hannah tells Leo about the red book. [F]
2 Hannah is sure that she can trust Leo. ☐
3 The assistant in the shop shows Hannah a pair of earrings. ☐
4 Leo and Mr Miller see Hannah in the mirror. ☐
5 Hannah feels sick in her cabin because of the stormy sea. ☐
6 Hannah learns that Mr Miller has stolen money from customers in England and America. ☐
7 Hannah thinks her father is in danger in New York. ☐
8 The sisters tell Leo where Hannah's cabin is. ☐

LOOKING FORWARD

6 What do you think? Who will meet Hannah when she arrives in New York?

her mother ☐ her father ☐ Alfie ☐
Marnie ☐ nobody ☐

Chapter 10

Lost at sea

As the passengers returned to their cabins, everyone was talking about the terrible news. Some people were crying.

'My cousin was on the *Titanic*,' Hannah heard one woman say, 'with her children.'

Everyone got ready to leave the *Andromeda*. Hannah and Leo said goodbye.

'I'll wait for you,' said Leo. 'I'll see you when you come through the Immigration Station.'

'Don't wait, Leo. Look at all these people – it's going to take hours,' said Hannah. 'Let's meet later or at the White Star office tomorrow – at ten.'

'All right,' said Leo. 'Here's the address of a hotel in Wall Street. One of the ship's officers said it was clean and cheap. I'm going to stay there – you could stay there too. And here, take this.' He gave her a wallet. 'There's twenty dollars inside. You may need it.'

'Thank you, Leo,' said Hannah. 'You've been good to me.'

She watched him leave the *Andromeda*.

Hannah left the ship with the third class travellers. They had to pass through the Immigration Station on Ellis Island.

They waited in a line in front of the immigration desk. The line moved slowly. After two hours, Hannah reached the front. The immigration officer asked her name and age. When she told him she was only sixteen and she was travelling alone, he sent her to a special waiting room. The other people in the waiting room looked very ill or very poor.

'Why are we here?' Hannah asked one of the women.

'They're going to send us back,' she cried, and she looked angrily at her husband. He was very thin and looked unwell. 'We should have waited until he was better.'

'Or dead,' said the man unhappily.

Over the next three hours, more people came into the waiting room. Then an immigration officer started to call them out, one at a time. Finally, Hannah's name was called, and she was taken into another room. An officer sat behind a desk. Hannah sat on a wooden chair opposite him.

'Where are your parents?' the officer asked Hannah.

'They're already here. I'm joining them,' she said.

'What's their address in New York?'

'I don't know,' said Hannah. 'I have to meet my mother at the White Star office.'

'Do you have a letter from your parents?'

'No, I don't,' said Hannah.

'We can't allow a single young woman into the United States, with no money or family. Who will look after you?'

'But I *do* have some money,' said Hannah.

'How much?'

'Three pounds in English money,' said Hannah. 'And twenty American dollars.'

'I'm sorry,' said the officer. 'We'll have to send you back.'

Just then, the telephone rang. The officer answered it and spoke quietly for a couple of minutes. Then he put the phone down and said to Hannah, 'All right, Miss Frost. You are free to enter the United States.'

'Oh!' she said, and bravely asked, 'Why have you changed your mind?'

'I probably shouldn't tell you, but you have an important friend,' said the officer. 'That phone call was from Mr Zimmerman of Miller's Bank.'

Hannah walked out of the Immigration Station.

'Mr Zimmerman – of Miller's Bank?' she thought. How could she explain that? Had Leo just used the name of Miller's Bank to get her into the United States? Or *was* he working for Mr Miller? How did he know she was still on Ellis Island?

It was late in the afternoon now, and most of the *Andromeda* passengers had left hours before. Hannah got on a boat that took her from Ellis Island across to the city. She had seen photographs of New York, but they were nothing like the real thing. The buildings were so tall and close together. Hannah's family was somewhere among those buildings – but where?

Hannah got off the boat and asked a man where the White Star office was. It was not far away, and she found it easily. There were crowds of people outside. As she came closer, she saw they were looking at lists of names on the outside of the building. They were the names of passengers from the *Titanic* – the names of the people who were lost at sea.

Hannah looked under 'M' for Marnie Moran. It wasn't there. Neither was Grace Moran.

'Oh, thank God,' she said.

There were hundreds of names. And then Hannah's face went white. She went closer to the list. There, under 'F', was a name she knew very well – her own name, Hannah Frost.

Chapter 11

Alone again

The White Star office was still open. There was a noisy crowd inside. At one end of the room, men from the company sat behind a long desk. People were pushing forward, trying to speak to them.

When Hannah got to the front, she shouted to a man behind the desk, 'I'm looking for my mother. Her name is Mrs Violet Frost. Has she been here?'

'Was she a passenger?' asked the man.

'No,' said Hannah. 'She thought I was on the *Titanic*, but I wasn't. I've just arrived on the *Andromeda*.'

'I can't help you,' said the man. 'We're helping people with family who were on the *Titanic*.'

'Please let me explain,' said Hannah. 'My name is Hannah Frost. My name is on the list outside, but I wasn't actually on the ship – I missed it. And now my mother thinks I'm dead.'

'Well, she'll be happy to learn that you're alive,' said the man. 'Now, I have all these people to talk to.'

'Please, I just need to know if you've spoken to Mrs Violet Frost or Mr Alfie Frost,' said Hannah, but the man was already talking to someone else.

As Hannah turned away, another man behind the desk said, 'Frost? Yes, I remember the name. She was one of the first people here. She was asking about her daughter.'

'Yes, that's her!' said Hannah. 'When was she here?'

'She came several times in the first few days – but I haven't seen her since then.'

'Did she leave a message or an address?'

‘No,’ said the man. ‘There’s no message.’ And he turned to talk to the next person in the crowd.

Hannah walked through the dark streets. She was alone again, and didn’t know where she was going. She had the address of Leo’s hotel, but after his phone call, she didn’t trust him. She didn’t know where her family was. And now they thought she was dead.

Although she was tired, she checked to see if anyone was following her. She turned left up one street and right down another, stopping sometimes to let people pass. Finally, she went into a cheap hotel. She took a room, lay on the bed and soon fell asleep.

The next morning, noise from the busy streets outside and the smell of coffee woke Hannah. She dressed and went downstairs. People were having breakfast in the hotel dining room. Hannah sat at a small table by the window.

The waiter brought her eggs and coffee.

'Have you heard about a new bank that's opening soon?' she asked the waiter. 'Miller's Bank?'

'No, I haven't, but try on Wall Street,' said the waiter. 'That's where all the banks are. Someone there will know.'

The sun was shining above, but the streets were dark under the tall buildings. Wall Street was full of people in suits walking to work. Hannah went into a bank. There was an information desk, and she asked about the new bank.

'The opening[18] of Miller's Bank is this afternoon at two o'clock,' said the woman behind the desk. 'The building is at the end of Wall Street. There'll be speeches[19] and drinks to welcome new customers. Anyone can go, I think.'

It was nearly ten o'clock. Hannah had over four hours to wait, and she walked along Wall Street. She had agreed to meet Leo at the White Star office at ten, but now she wanted to find her family on her own. It was possible that Leo was working for Mr Miller. She didn't want to lead him to her father.

She came to a church and went inside. It was empty, and she sat down to think. Perhaps her mother or Alfie would be at the opening. Her father wouldn't be there, she was sure – it would be too dangerous for him. She felt Mr Miller's red book in her coat pocket. Was she brave enough to stand up at the opening and tell people about it? She hoped so.

As the church bell sounded ten, she heard steps behind her on the stone floor. She turned, and there was Leo.

'Hannah,' he said, looking worried. 'I saw you walking up Wall Street from my hotel window. I was going to walk down to the White Star office. Didn't we agree to meet there?'

'Oh, you just saw me by chance, did you?' said Hannah angrily. 'I don't think so, Leo. I think you and Mr Miller have followed me since I left Ellis Island.'

'No, you're wrong,' said Leo. 'Why do you think that?'

'When I was at Ellis Island yesterday,' said Hannah, 'they told me I had "an important friend – Mr Zimmerman of Miller's Bank".'

'Oh, I just said that to get you in,' said Leo. 'I waited for you for about two hours at Ellis Island, but you didn't come out. I came across to New York and telephoned the Immigration Station from my hotel. I asked where you were. They said they were planning to send you back to England. So I said I was with Miller's Bank and you were coming to the bank opening. I said Mr Miller was a good friend of your family.'

'You can explain everything, can't you?' said Hannah.

He smiled.

'Well, you've found me now,' said Hannah. 'I'm going to the bank opening this afternoon.'

'I'll go with you,' said Leo. 'Let's take a walk, and then I'll buy you lunch.'

Chapter 12

Miller's Bank, New York

By two o'clock, the main room at the new bank was full. There weren't enough seats, and people were standing at the sides. They were here to put their money in this new bank and they were talking excitedly. Hannah and Leo were in seats near the back, on the right.

'Ssh!' people said. Mr Miller was coming in with some other men who all looked important. They stood at the front.

'Ladies and gentlemen, thank you all for coming,' started Mr Miller. 'It's wonderful to be here in Wall Street, the home of so many great banks. This is a great day for me and for Miller's Bank. And for you too, I hope!'

Everyone laughed.

Leo kept looking around the room. 'Do you think your mother or father will come?' he whispered to Hannah. 'I can't see them.'

'No,' said Hannah. 'It would be too dangerous.'

'Ssh!' said a man in front of them.

'I'm going to look for them,' said Leo. He stood up and walked towards the front, looking back at the faces.

Mr Miller continued his speech, describing the history of his bank in England.

'Now, some of you may have heard about some trouble at our bank last year,' said Mr Miller. 'A man called Henry Frost used to work for me. He was the bank's most brilliant accountant[20]. We had worked together for ten years. I trusted him. But I am sorry to say that he became jealous of me. He decided to start his own bank *inside* Miller's Bank!'

Everyone laughed again.

'His bank was unusual,' said Mr Miller. 'Customers put money in, and he took it out!'

'Oh, that's a lie!' said Hannah loudly.

People turned around and looked at her.

Leo had now reached the front of the room. He and Mr Miller looked at each other for a moment, and Mr Miller continued. 'Luckily, my assistant, Mr Leo Zimmerman, realised what was happening.'

'Leo!' cried Hannah, standing up. Now she knew the truth. People started to whisper all around the room.

Mr Miller's voice got louder. 'Before the police in England could catch Mr Frost, he escaped and came here, to New York. We hope to catch him soon. But Mr Frost is not the only thief in his family! His daughter is a thief too. And I believe she is with us now. Am I right, Mr Zimmerman?'

'Yes,' said Leo, looking at Hannah. 'That's her.'

Hannah looked around the room. Two police officers were coming towards her.

'A thief?' she cried. 'What do you mean?'

'Mr Zimmerman,' said Mr Miller, smiling at Leo. 'Did you find this young lady in my cabin on the *Andromeda* eight days ago?'

'Yes, I did,' said Leo.

'And was she trying to steal from that cabin?'

'Yes, she was,' said Leo, and he turned to the police officers. 'If you look in her pocket, you'll find Mr Miller's wallet!'

'Please take this young lady to the police station,' said Mr Miller to the police officers.

Hannah knew what she had to do. She wasn't nervous now. She was angry.

'Yes, it's true,' she shouted confidently. 'I was in Mr Miller's cabin. And I found this.' She held up the red book with the date '1911'.

Mr Miller stopped smiling.

Hannah continued. 'This book shows that Mr Miller stole money from his customers at Miller's Bank. It shows that Mr Frost – my father – is innocent and Mr Miller is the thief!'

Everyone was talking loudly now.

Leo came towards Hannah. 'I'll take that book,' he said.

Suddenly a young man jumped in front of Leo and stopped him. It was Alfie.

'No, you won't!' he shouted.

'Alfie!' cried Hannah.

'OK, nobody move,' shouted one of the police officers. Everyone was quiet again. 'We'd like to speak to Mr Miller, Mr Zimmerman and this young lady at the police station.'

'Get out of my way!' shouted Leo, as he pushed between two lines of seats, climbing over people. The police tried to stop him as he got to the door, but he ran out into the street. One of the officers ran after him.

* * *

'Hannah, you're a very brave girl,' said Mr Frost to his daughter. 'Thanks to you, the world knows I am innocent.'

It was three days later, and the Frost family was sitting down to eat in the best restaurant in New York.

'The last two weeks have been like a bad dream!' said Hannah.

‘You’ve had a terrible time, my love,’ said Mrs Frost.

‘We’ve all had a terrible time,’ said Hannah, kissing first her mother and then her father.

‘When I saw your name on the list of lost passengers, my whole world died,’ said Mrs Frost, taking her daughter’s hand. ‘I’m just so happy you’re alive!’

The waiter came with their drinks.

‘Will we ever see Marnie again, do you think?’ asked Hannah.

‘I hope not,’ said Mrs Frost. ‘How could she leave you alone? She’s known you since you were a baby.’

‘She must be alive – her name wasn’t on the list of dead passengers,’ said Mr Frost. ‘I don’t think Grace was so lucky, though.’

Hannah wanted to cry. Grace was only a girl, just like her.

'Mr Miller's plan nearly worked, didn't it?' said Alfie. 'He wanted the police to keep Hannah in the police station for stealing Mr Miller's wallet. Then he thought Mother and Father would come out of their hiding place to help her—'

'—and the police would throw me in prison,' said Mr Frost. 'Yes, it nearly worked. But it *didn't*, because you took that book from Mr Miller's cabin, Hannah.'

'And Leo was following me all the time,' said Hannah. 'Oh, Father! He was so nice to me. I almost trusted him, but I was never quite sure. What do you think will happen to Leo?'

'They'll take him back to England with Mr Miller. There'll be a trial, and they'll go to prison,' said Mr Frost. 'We'll have to go back too. They'll need us all at the trial.'

'What will we do then?' asked Hannah.

'Your mother and I quite like this city,' said Mr Frost. 'And a Wall Street bank has already offered me a job. We want to start a new life here. What do you think?'

'Yes!' said Hannah and Alfie together. They all held up their glasses.

'To our new life,' said Mr Frost.

Hannah, Alfie and their mother smiled. 'To our new life!' they all said.

LOOKING BACK

1. Check your answers to *Looking forward* on page 61.

ACTIVITIES

2. Match the two parts of the sentences.

1 Leo tells Hannah he going to stay in [d]
2 Before he leaves the ship, Leo gives Hannah [ ]
3 An immigration officer sends Hannah to [ ]
4 The immigration officer receives a phone call from [ ]
5 People outside the White Star office are looking at [ ]
6 When Hannah looks at the lists, she sees [ ]

a her own name.
b Mr Leo Zimmerman of Miller's Bank.
c a wallet with twenty dollars in it.
d a cheap hotel in Wall Street.
e a special waiting room.
f lists of *Titanic* passengers who were lost at sea.

3. Are the sentences true (*T*) or false (*F*)?

1 There is a message at the White Star office for Hannah. [F]
2 Only people with invitations can go to the opening of Miller's Bank. [ ]
3 Hannah meets Leo at the White Star office at ten o'clock. [ ]
4 Hannah thinks her father will be at the bank opening. [ ]
5 Leo says he saw Hannah from his hotel window. [ ]
6 Leo says he never telephoned the Immigration Station. [ ]

4 Underline the correct words in each sentence.

1 Hannah goes to the bank opening *alone* / *with Leo*.
2 Leo *looks for* / *finds* Hannah's parents at the opening.
3 *Leo* / *Mr Miller* makes a speech at the opening.
4 Hannah learns the truth: Leo has been working for *Mr Miller* / *Mr Frost*.
5 *Alfie* / *Mr Frost* stops Leo from getting the red book.
6 Mr Frost thinks Grace is probably *alive* / *dead*.
7 Mr Frost says Leo will go to prison in *America* / *England*.
8 Hannah and her family decide to start a new life in *New York* / *Southampton*.

5 Complete the summary with the names and words in the box.

Hannah (x3)	Mr Frost	Mr and Mrs Frost	
~~Leo~~	Mr Miller	everyone	the police (x2)

This was Mr Miller's plan: 1 ....Leo.... gave a wallet to 2 .... The wallet belonged to 3 .... Mr Miller hoped that 4 .... would keep 5 .... in the police station for stealing the wallet. Then he hoped that 6 .... would come to help her, and 7 .... would throw 8 .... into prison. But the plan didn't work because 9 .... had taken the red book from his cabin, and she stood up at the bank and told 10 .... all about it.

Glossary

[1]**innocent** (page 8) *adjective* if you are innocent of a crime, then you did not do it

[2]**rent** (page 8) *noun* the money you pay to live in a house that someone else owns

[3]**accounts** (page 13) *noun* a record of the money that a company has received or paid

[4]**customer** (page 14) *noun* a person who buys things from a shop or does business with a company

[5]**unconscious** (page 15) *adjective* not thinking or feeling anything, perhaps because of taking a drug or being hit on the head

[6]**thief** (page 20) *noun* someone who steals things

[7]**servant** (page 21) *noun* someone who works and lives in someone else's house, doing their cooking and cleaning

[8]**docks** (page 31) *noun* the place where ships stop and things are taken off or put on

[9]**cabin** (page 31) *noun* a small room to sleep in on a ship

[10]**list** (page 32) *noun* a lot of names or numbers written one below the other

[11]**deck** (page 38) *noun* one of the floors of a ship

[12]**captain** (page 46) *noun* the most important officer on a ship

[13]**trial** (page 50) *noun* the time when a group of people come together to hear information about a crime and decide if a person is innocent or not

[14]**interest rate** (page 52) *noun* the amount of extra money you earn from keeping your money in a bank

[15]**trust** (page 52) *verb* to believe that someone is honest

[16]**ladies and gentlemen** (page 53) *expression* a way of starting to talk to a group of men and women

[17]**immigration** (page 59) *adjective* to do with checking people who are arriving in a country

[18]**opening** (page 68) *noun* the time when a company or shop starts doing business for the first time

[19]**speech** (page 68) *noun* a talk given to a group of people

[20]**accountant** (page 71) *noun* a person whose job is to keep accounts